UNBROKEN:
FROM COMA TO CONQUEROR

Nike Okeke

Book Description

Unbroken: My Journey from Coma to Conqueror is a memoir of hope, strength, and the will to live. In simple, heartfelt words, I share how a sudden, life-changing incident turned my world upside down—and how I fought back, step by step, to reclaim my life.

This book takes you on a journey from the dark moments in a hospital bed to the triumphant day I walked out on my own two feet, all while inspiring you to believe that no setback is too big to overcome. You will read about the tough therapies, the magical visits from my children, and even a surprising dream that hinted at my future.

Every page is filled with courage, determination, and a message of never giving up. If you are looking for a story that lights a fire in your heart and reminds you that every challenge is a chance to grow, then this is the book for you. Let Unbroken show you that even in our hardest moments, hope can lead us to a new beginning.

Contents

Foreword
by Adeyemi C. Aderinto

There are moments in life that split your existence into *before* and *after*. For me, it was a phone call at 3 a.m.

When I saw my sister's husband's name on the screen, a cold dread settled in my chest. We rarely spoke, and no one calls at that hour with good news. Before I even picked up, my heart was already racing, as if it understood something my mind wasn't ready to accept.

When I picked up, his voice was flat, heavy with the weight of words he didn't want to say.

"It's Nike," he began.

That was all it took for my world to tilt. He kept talking and explaining what had happened and how the doctors had tried their best, but I was no longer fully there. My mind clung to one question, the only thing that mattered in that moment:

"Is she alive?"

"Yes," he replied.

I ended the call.

My wife, now awake, saw the look on my face and understood without needing details. We fell to our knees, not out of ritual but sheer desperation. Our prayers weren't polished or poetic; they were raw, urgent cries from a place deeper than fear.

The neighbors heard us. My cries weren't just sounds; they were the raw echoes of sorrow and desperation intertwining. It wasn't the earth that trembled, it was me! Shaken from the inside out.

Morning brought no peace. When I called back, the doctors spoke cautiously:

"She might live," they said, as if hope was something fragile, we had to handle with care. Then they told us about another patient—a man in the same hospital, recently declared brain-dead. His family had just agreed to take him off life support. I knew why they were sharing that story. They were preparing us.

But we weren't ready.

We prayed harder. We called again.

"She might not be brain dead, but she could be paralyzed."

Then: "She's breathing on her own."

"She might be able to talk."

"She's moving her toe."

"She might be able to walk."

Hope didn't come all at once. It came in fragments, small enough to hold but big enough to keep us going.

A year and a half later, my sister traveled to Nigeria- by herself!

That journey wasn't just hers; it was ours. A story of fear, faith, and the fragile thread of hope that refused to snap.

As you turn pages and read through, I invite you to journey with us, not just through the events, but through the emotions, the uncertainties, and the quiet miracles that emerged when hope seemed out of reach.

This isn't just my sister's story. It is a huge part of my story, and it is a testament to what's possible when life says *no,* and faith says *not yet.*

So, welcome to our story

  -Adeyemi Chris Aderinto

Introduction: A Journey of Hope and Resilience

Every journey begins with a single step, though we rarely know where that step will lead us. For me, the journey that shaped this book began unexpectedly, on an ordinary day, when life as I knew it was turned upside down. I left for work, as I had done countless times before, unaware that it would be nearly two months before I returned home. During that time, I encountered challenges I never could have anticipated and gained lessons that reshaped me forever.

While I never anticipated the challenges ahead, this is not just the story of my survival, though surviving was, at times, an immense feat. It is the story of how I found hope in the darkest moments, how resilience became my guide when the future seemed uncertain, and how I rediscovered the power of faith, love, and human connection. It's the story of how the unexpected can bring us to the brink of despair but also lift us toward transformation.

I spent weeks in the hospital, confined to a bed, with tubes and machines sustaining my body while my spirit fought to heal. It was a time of great physical and emotional struggle, but it was also a time of reflection. I had to confront my vulnerability, and push against the limitations of my body, discovering depths of resilience I never knew I had. Yet, through it all, I discovered strength, not only within myself but also in the unwavering support of those around me, in the quiet moments of grace, and in the steadfast belief that my story was far from over.

This book is a testament to the incredible power of perseverance, the inner strength we all possess, even when we feel broken or lost. It's about the ways we can rise, again and again, no matter how many times life knocks us down. It's about finding hope in the smallest moments and about the healing that happens not just physically but, in the heart, and soul.

As you turn these pages, you'll walk beside me through moments of unwavering faith and determination. You'll witness the struggles, the small victories, and the unexpected lessons that came with them. More importantly, you'll see how even the hardest challenges can lead to unexpected blessings.

This journey is a testament to the strength we all carry within us, even when we don't realize it. It's a reminder that in our weakest moments, we often discover our greatest resilience.

As you walk this path with me, I hope you find your own spark of hope, strength, and transformation, no matter where life's journey has taken you. Whether you're facing your own battles, supporting someone you love, or simply seeking to understand the depth of human endurance, I hope my story inspires you.

Life is unpredictable, but if there's one thing I've learned, and one thing I hope you take from these pages, it's this: there is always hope, even when the road ahead is uncertain.

May my story be a reminder that we are never alone in our struggles, that resilience is within us all, and that with hope and faith, we can overcome even the most daunting of challenges.

This is my journey of hope, faith, tenacity, and determination. I invite you to share in it, and through it, to find your own strength to keep going with hope for a better outcome.

Chapter 1:

The Day Everything Changed

July 22, 2022

An Ordinary Day?

It was a Friday morning like any other—ordinary in every way. But it was also July 22, 2022, a day I barely lived, yet one I will never forget. The sun, still groggy from its rise, cast faint shadows as I stepped outside. My routine was as predictable as clockwork; another hurried ride to work, another day I thought would blend seamlessly into the blur of countless others before it.

If you had asked me that morning, I would have assured you I'd be home by evening—perhaps unwinding with a movie alongside my kids, tackling overdue chores, or finally catching up on some much-needed rest. There was no reason to believe the day would be anything but ordinary.

But life rarely announces its twists. It doesn't signal when it's about to veer off the rails, leaving everything you know behind.

If I could go back, I'd look for signs, some small clue of the storm ahead. But, of course, I can't. All I know is that one moment, life was routine, and the next, it was utterly unrecognizable.

The Moment Everything Changed

I don't quite remember, but my work colleagues recounted the laughter that filled the room that morning. We were all in good spirits, sharing stories to lighten the mood before the real work began.

Then it happened.

One moment, I was laughing; the next, my body betrayed me.

I collapsed.

I went unconscious.

Some of my coworkers said they thought I was playing a joke, falling dramatically to get a laugh. But it quickly became apparent that this was no joke. I can imagine the frantic voices around me and the panic in the air as people rushed to my side.

I was no longer truly there—just a motionless body on the floor. The laughter that had filled the room moments earlier was replaced by stunned silence. My colleagues, their faces frozen in shock, stood paralyzed before frantic shouts for help broke through the heavy air.

"Is this real? What's happening?" I imagine those questions racing through their minds as they worked to keep me alive.

Rob, one of my coworkers who witnessed the entire event, later told me what happened in those terrifying moments. My eyes were wide open, staring blankly ahead. When the doctor on site arrived quickly and touched my eyeballs to check for any response, I didn't blink. I just lay there, completely still, unresponsive to everything around me.

Life's Fragility and Vulnerability

There's a certain arrogance we carry when life is predictable. We move through our routines as if we are invincible, as if tomorrow will always come. But this whole experience thought me just how fragile life really is.

Everything we take for granted; our health, our independence, our ability to move through the world, can be taken from us in an instant. I never thought an ordinary day could spiral so abruptly, that my body could betray me without the slightest warning. But it did—and in that instant, I was powerless to resist it.

It's startling how life can shift in an instant, the illusion of control shattered by the reality of unpredictability. One minute, everything is fine. The next, the world narrows to survival, to the counts of your breath, the beating of your heart, things we seldom think about until they are at risk. In that fragile moment, you realize how quickly the familiar can dissolve into chaos, exposing the raw vulnerability of being human.

Life is not a guarantee; it's a gift we're given moment by moment. What we often dismiss as mundane; a boring meeting, a walk to the car, the simplest tasks, can vanish without warning. We are fragile creatures, holding onto the belief that we'll always be okay until suddenly, we are not.

That experience taught me a harsh but necessary lesson: Never take anything for granted. When we do, we miss the quiet beauty woven into the everyday; the joy of simply being alive. Life's fragility, in all its humbling power, reminds us to cherish each moment as it comes.

The truth is, we are not invincible. And it's only when life shakes us that we see how delicate and precious, it really is.

The Race to Save Me

I've pieced together the events from what others have told me. My coworkers announced a code blue as soon as they noticed I was unresponsive. The medical doctor on-site ran from another unit and ran as fast as he could to the unit where I was supposed to be working when he heard the overhead page.

Every second mattered. Time seemed to stretch as they waited for the emergency team to arrive, but my coworkers didn't waste a moment. They worked tirelessly to keep me stable, following every protocol we had all learned in the countless drills we had practiced but which none of us ever thought we would have to use on one of our own.

As I lay there, unconscious, they were my lifeline. Their quick thinking and immediate actions were vital to my survival.

I was first taken to the emergency center in our small town. They did everything to keep me stable. Odessa (another co-worker and friend of mine) stayed with me the whole time, waiting by my side until I was transported by air ambulance to the Foothills Medical Hospital, barely clinging to life. I hovered in a space between life and death.

In those moments, as machines sustained my body and doctors rushed to uncover answers, I was oblivious to the whirlwind around me. Suspended between life and death, I drifted into a space where time and awareness ceased to exist.

My husband was working ten hours away, far from the chaos that had upended our lives. I was supposed to be the one holding things together at home, the steady hand, the comforting presence for our children. But then I'd gone unconscious, whisked away to the city in a rush, leaving a terrifying void behind. No one could say when or even if I would be back.

Chiki stepped in, my steadfast friend and coworker, though I can only imagine the weight of uncertainty she carried. Her task was simple in theory but unbearably heavy in reality: to soothe the children, to make them believe that life was still every day when, in truth, nothing had ever been further from it.

She went home to them, and despite the storm brewing inside her, she seemed contained. *"Your mum has to get some blood transfusions at the hospital,"* she told them. *"She might be there for a couple of days."*

She chose the words wisely, but they still felt like throwing a blanket over a shattered window; enough to shield them from the sharp edges of reality, but unable to mend the break beneath.

Chiki didn't know how to tell them the truth. How could she? How do you look into the eyes of children who have always believed their mother to be unshakable and tell them she might never come home? That this day might be the dividing line between the life they had known and an uncertain future? My daughter, Victoria, was only 12, but even at that age, she could see past the carefully chosen words meant to protect her. *"I knew it was more than what Chiki told us,"*

Victoria later admitted. *"I knew something was wrong when Chiki asked for Daddy's phone number."*

Victoria knew. She felt the weight of the unspoken truth pressing against the silence, lurking beneath the reassurances.

And Chiki, how did she bear it?

How did she carry the crushing pressure of pretending? Of holding her fears at bay while weaving a delicate shield of calm around my children? Did she feel the weight of every word crushing down her? Did she lie awake that night, haunted by the innocence in their eyes, by the knowledge that the truth would come crashing down on them soon enough?

She must have carried so much in those moments, protecting them not just from what was happening but from the fear that would consume them upon knowing. Shielding them, even as she, too, was barely holding on.

Chiki did more than just keep the children at ease, she stayed. She slept in my house with them, keeping their routines as normal as possible while waiting alongside them.

Meanwhile, my husband embarked on a long, anxious drive from his workplace to the hospital where I had been admitted, each mile stretching the weight of his worry. He was rushing to a wife he wasn't sure he would find conscious, leaving the children in Chiki's care with no clear roadmap for what would come next.

From my hospital bed, I was unaware of all this. But looking back, I can imagine the scene with painful clarity. The quiet house. My children waiting for me to walk through the door like I always had. Chiki doing her best to keep their hope alive while facing the possibility that I might never return. It's a strange, bittersweet thing to think about now. Chiki's kindness and courage shielded my children and provided them with a sense of safety, even if only for a short while. But knowing they were waiting, hoping, and asking questions she couldn't answer still breaks my heart in ways I struggle to express.

A Glimpse of Gratitude

When I think back to that day, I can't help but feel a surge of gratitude. Gratitude not only for the doctors and nurses who worked so tirelessly to keep me alive but also for the people who stood by me when I couldn't stand for myself. It wasn't just the skilled medical team or the advanced technology that was working to save me; it was the people around me, my family and friends, their love, their care, and their belief in my recovery. As I lay there unconscious, it was their hope, their prayers, and their unwavering support that began to stitch together the pieces of my life.

This was the beginning of a new chapter in my life, one that would be marked by profound lessons in resilience, inner strength, and the power of human connection.

Reflections and Lessons to Consider

It's easy to think we are invincible when life feels predictable, but one shift in circumstance can change everything:

- Cherish the ordinary. Each moment: each interaction, each small thing we tend to overlook, is a gift. The very routines we think are mundane could one day become the foundation of our memories, reminding us of how far we've come. Don't wait for a life-altering moment to start appreciating what you have today. Start cherishing the little things now, because they are the building blocks of a fulfilling life.

- Don't put off until tomorrow what you can do today. Life is unpredictable; every moment is a gift. Act now with faith and courage. "Treasure each moment, tell the people you love how much they mean to you. Live fully in the present. No matter how small or large, each day is a gift that deserves our appreciation.

- If today is the only gift you have, what will you do with it?

No One Knows the Next Second

No one knows what comes next,
Not the time, the twist, or the text.
A moment can change the sky above,
Turn fear to strength, hate to love.

One second, we stumble and fall,
The next, we rise and stand tall.
Life moves fast, like winds that roam,
But even storms can lead us home.

Don't wait for perfect days to start,
Hope begins inside your heart.
A smile, a step, a word so kind
Can shift the soul and free the mind.

The clock keeps ticking, soft and bold,
And none of us know what it holds.
But here you are; alive, awake,
With breath to give and steps to take.

Dream out loud, forgive the past,
Love like today could be your last.
And trust that even in the unknown,
You're never lost, you're never alone.

Chapter 2:

Waking in Darkness

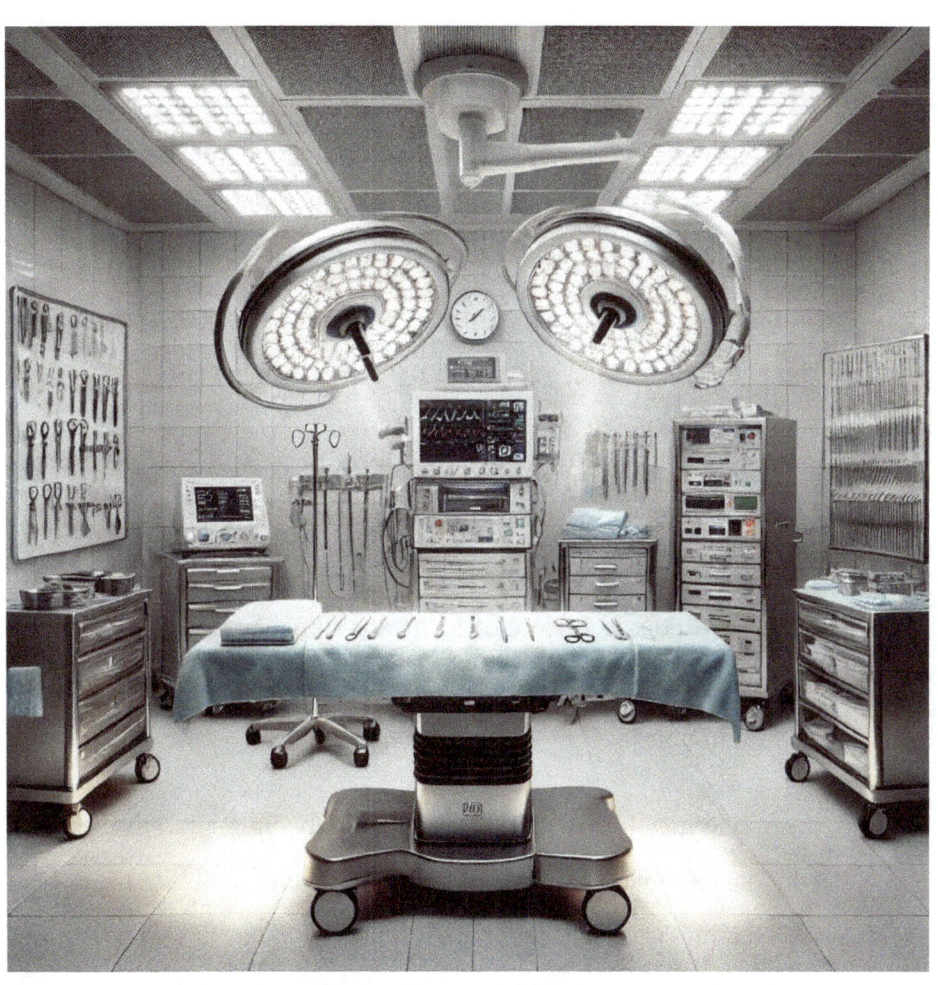

The Fight for a Fragile Hope

It had been over ten hours since I arrived at the hospital unconscious, slipping further away with every minute. Inside my skull, two brain aneurysms waged war, one already ruptured, unleashing devastation in its wake. Blood pooled where it shouldn't, creating unbearable pressure that pushed me closer to paralysis and death. I later read in my neurologist's summary that my Glasgow Coma Scale score was just 4 out of 15 —a grim number in a system designed to measure the difference between life, death, and the space in between.

For those unfamiliar, the **Glasgow Coma Scale (GCS)** is a tool that doctors and nurses use to assess a person's level of consciousness after a brain injury. It measures three key functions: eye movement, speech, and motor response. A score of **15** means someone is fully alert, while a **3** indicates a deep coma or brain death. A score of **8 or below** signals severe brain injury.

A score of **4** meant I was unresponsive, barely clinging to life, entirely dependent on machines and medical intervention. I wasn't aware, wasn't feeling, wasn't present. There was only silence. A score that low often makes doctors exchange quiet glances, the kind that speak of unspoken truths. The prognosis is rarely good. And yet, even at **4**, something deep within me refused to surrender.

But while I was locked in unconsciousness, my husband was living through a nightmare wide awake.

He had been on the road for nine long hours, racing toward the hospital with nothing but dread and desperation keeping him company. The miles stretched endlessly before him; each one filled with unbearable questions. Would I still be alive when he arrived? Would doctors ask him to make the impossible decision to let me go? Was our life together ending right here, right now?

When he finally arrived, the medical team was waiting. They had run every test and studied every scan. Now, they needed his consent. He was the decision-maker.

The prognosis was bleak. The doctors explained the extent of the rupture, the blood that had flooded my brain for hours. They spoke of the emergency surgery that might offer me the slimmest chance of survival; but also the risks. I might not wake up. And if I did, I could be paralyzed, unable to speak, stripped of my memories; a shell of the person I once was.

I can only imagine my husband standing in the sterile hospital room, drowning in impossible choices. Should he fight for me, knowing the battle ahead could leave me broken? Or should he let me go, sparing me the pain of waking to a life I might no longer recognize?

He called my brother; his voice weighed down by the burden of what he had just heard. When he explained the situation, my brother didn't hesitate. *"Do the surgery,"* he said firmly. *"Don't think twice about it."*

And just like that, the decision was made. My husband passed the final word to the surgeons: *"Go ahead."*

Exhausted and emotionally drained, he left the hospital that night, knowing there was nothing more he could do but wait and hope.

A Terrifying Morning

The following day brought an unexpected and unsettling shock. When my husband returned to my hospital room, expecting to find me post-surgery, he instead found me precisely as he had left me, lying motionless in the bed. The surgery hadn't happened.

Confused, he moved closer. The machines beeped steadily, the only sound in the room. He reached out and applied pressure to my foot, something he had seen doctors do the day before as part of their assessments. The previous day, I had reacted to the pain. My foot had flinched; a small but vital sign of life.

Today, there was nothing. No reaction. No movement.

Panic surged through him. He rushed into the hallway, his voice urgent as he found a nurse and explained what had happened. As he was speaking, a surgeon approached, and my husband wasted no time repeating the terrifying discovery.

The surgeon acted immediately. He stepped into the room, applied pressure to my foot, and waited. Nothing happened. No response came. No reflex. Something had changed overnight, and not for the better.

Without hesitation, the surgeon turned to the nurse and issued the command that sent everything into motion: *"Get the operating room ready for emergency surgery."*

Now, it was indeed a race against time.

A Battle in the Operating Room

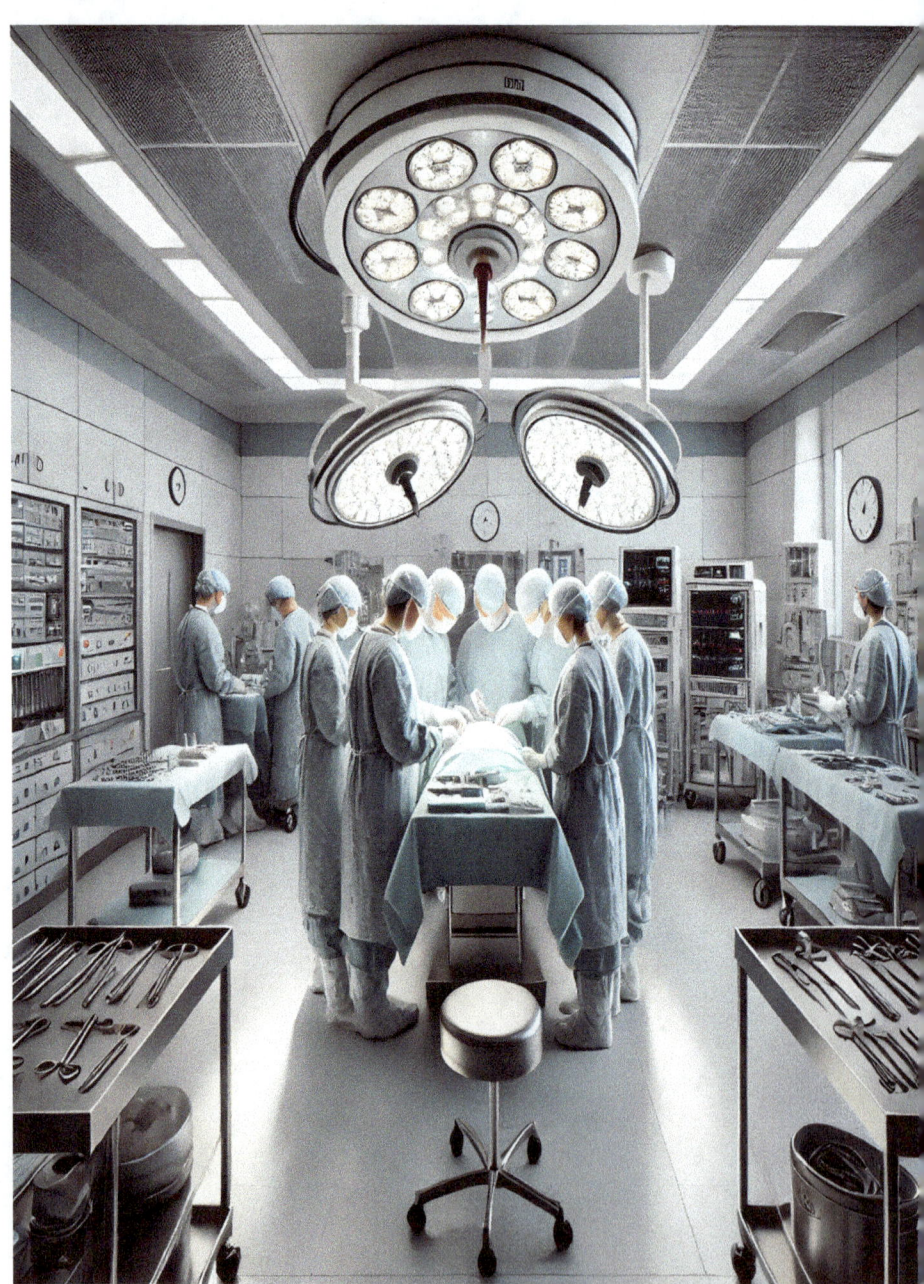

The surgical team mobilized quickly, knowing the situation had turned even more dire than before. Every passing second mattered. As the doors to the operating room swung shut behind me, my husband was left standing outside, feeling more powerless than ever. The glimmer of hope he had been clinging to now felt even more fragile.

For my family and friends, the hours that followed were agonizing. Scattered across different places, they waited, separately, yet united in hope. After waiting for a while, my husband left the hospital; he needed to get some rest. My family, miles away, held their breath, clinging to their phones, desperate for any updates.

Dr Okeke Director... 📹 📞 ⋮

was there. Will go back again tonight though. So will see them tomorrow morning
11:10 PM

Just talked to them at the hospital. She is still in surgery. Will call again after some time. I need to try get some sleep
11:12 PM

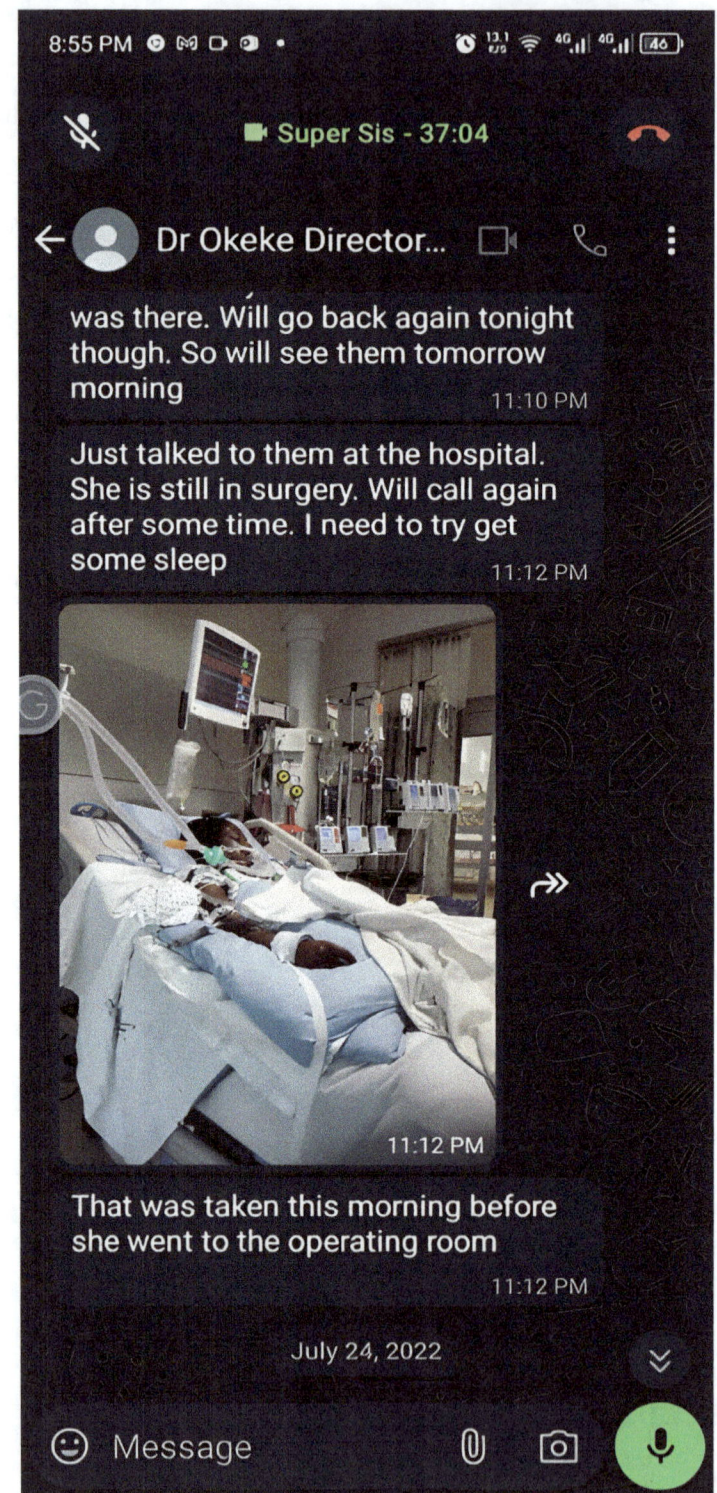

11:12 PM

That was taken this morning before she went to the operating room
11:12 PM

July 24, 2022

☺ Message 📎 📷 🎤

The surgery was my best chance. But it was also a leap of faith, a gamble on the slimmest margins of hope.

When it was over, I remained unconscious. The doctors had done all they could, repairing the rupture and stabilizing me, but now, it was up to my body to heal. I hovered between life and death for nearly two weeks.

For my family, those weeks were a relentless test of endurance and faith. My hospital room became a sacred space of whispered prayers and quiet vigil. My husband sat beside me, day after day, holding my hand as if the warmth of his touch alone could pull me back. He watched the monitors, searching for any sign, any shift in the numbers that might mean I was coming back.

Every day, the doctors monitored me, but their words were cautious. The surgery had been a success, but the damage was extensive. *Even if she wakes up,* they warned, *there are no guarantees.* I might never move. I might never speak. I might not recognize the people I loved.

The waiting stretched endlessly. But then, something changed...

A Whisper of Awakening

The first moments were faint, slipping between reality and dream. At times, I would open my eyes to blurred figures hovering nearby; nurses and doctors, moving like shadows. Other times, I drifted back into darkness before I could make sense of anything.

But then, a moment of clarity. I opened my eyes, and there he was, my husband. He stood beside me, phone in hand, his face alight with something that looked like disbelief and joy all at once. And then, through the haze, I heard his voice.

"This is a miracle, Mehn."

Later, I saw the video he recorded that day. Watching it made me smile. A beautiful, undeniable reminder of just how much love surrounded me in that fragile state. I had survived. I was waking up. The fight was far from over, but I was still here.

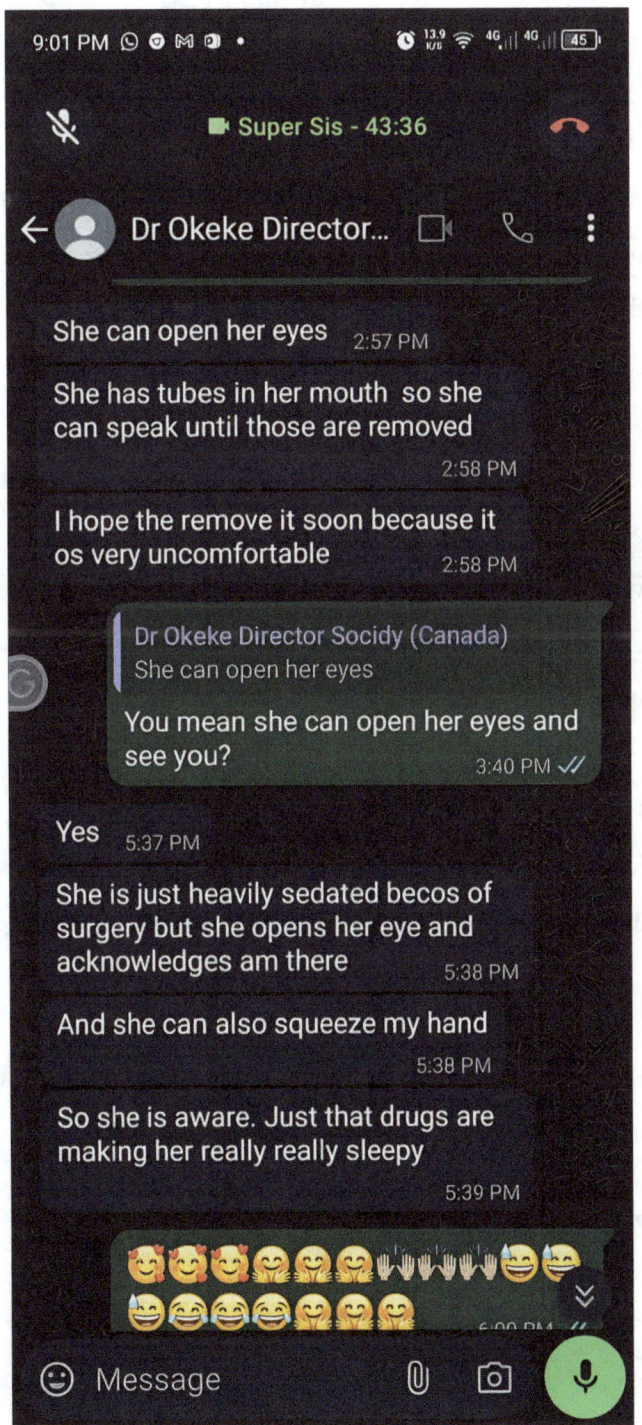

Reflection and Lessons to Consider

- Life's toughest moments often force us into decisions with no clear answers. But the courage to move forward in the face of fear, to choose hope over despair, can make all the difference. Even when the road is uncertain, taking the first step can sometimes be the only thing that matters.

- No one goes through life's darkest times alone. The people who stand by us, hold our hands, and offer prayers and encouragement can help carry us through when we feel like we have nothing left to give.

- Hope can be fragile, but it is also unyielding. It's easy to lose faith when faced with overwhelming odds, but hope can sustain us when everything else feels uncertain. In the darkest moments, hope can light the way forward.

- Faith as small as a mustard seed can break through the hardest ground. Keep believing. Keep holding on.

A Fragile Hope

In shadows deep where silence grows,
Where sorrow sleeps and no light show,
A flicker stirs, so faint, so small
A whisper rising through it all.

It trembles in the cold night air,
A dream, a prayer, a silent dare.
Not loud, not bold, not fully grown,
But brave enough to stand alone.

The winds may howl, the nights may bite,
But hope will clutch the edge of light.
It bends, it breaks, it weeps in pain,
Yet finds the strength to rise again.

The fight is not with sword or shield,
But hearts that never choose to yield.
Each step is slow, each breath a test,
Yet hope keeps beating in the chest.

For though the world may turn away,
And skies may darken every day,
Still hope, so fragile, finds a way
To bloom beneath the feet of clay.

Chapter 3:
The First Moments of Awareness

During those moments when I drifted in and out of consciousness, I was aware that I was lying in a hospital bed. Strangely, I felt no urgency to piece together how I had ended up there. Instead, a quiet sense of calm settled over me as if the answers could wait, as if that was the moment for me to break free from all the worries and lie in peace.

There was a moment when I opened my eyes but wasn't sure if I was sleeping or awake. The line between dreams and reality blurred. It was only when I tried to lift my arms and found them pinned down that I realized I was awake. Yet, inexplicably, I remained calm. Deep down, I just knew I was safe.

The soft sound of footsteps drew my attention as a nurse entered the room. Her movements were deliberate and careful, her expression exuding a quiet confidence that only comes from years of experience. She noticed my feeble attempt to move and immediately came to my side.

"It's okay," she said softly, adjusting the tubes and IVs attached to my body.

I wanted to respond, to ask why my hands were restrained, but as I tried to speak, the tube in my throat prevented any sound. Instinctively, I reached for it, desperate to remove the foreign object, but the restraints around my wrists stopped me.

The nurse placed a reassuring hand on mine. "We had to restrain your hands because you were trying to remove the tube that's helping you breathe," she explained in a soothing tone. "But I assure you, I will loosen them if you can promise not to try again. That tube needs to stay in place for now."

I nodded, signaling my understanding. True to her word, she adjusted the restraints, giving me just enough freedom to move my hands slightly. It wasn't much, but it was enough.

I let myself relax. The nurse smiled. She didn't leave immediately after adjusting my IV or checking the monitors. She stayed for a moment, making sure I was okay. And in that moment, her presence felt like an anchor, tethering me to reality.

The Power of Trust

In that room, surrounded by machines and bound by my own body's limitations, I learned my first important lesson on this journey: the power of trust. When your body fails you, and your voice is silenced, trust becomes your lifeline. I had to trust the people around me; the nurses, the doctors, the surgeons, without knowing their names or their faces. I had to believe they knew what they were doing, that they had my best interests at heart.

I realized then that healing wasn't just about medicine or surgery; it was about surrender, about letting go of the need to control every moment and allowing others to carry you when you couldn't carry yourself.

It wasn't easy. I had spent my life in control; of my career, my family, my decisions, but now, all of that was gone. I couldn't even lift my arms. In that hospital bed, I was dependent on the very people I had trained alongside, the people I had once worked with as equals. Now, I had to trust that they would care for me as I had once cared for so many others.

Unexplainable Peace

The days blurred together. I drifted in and out of consciousness, caught between moments of sharp clarity and confusion. Sometimes, I would wake up with a strange sense of déjà vu, certain that I had lived the same moment before. Other times, I would wake with the stark realization that I was still trapped in this unfamiliar reality; the restraints around my wrists and the tube down my throat were a constant reminder.

But each time I woke, someone was there; a nurse, a doctor, a technician, a family member, a friend, someone who would calmly remind me where I was and why I needed to stay still. Their voices became my lifeline, their presence a reassurance that I wasn't alone.

It was during one of those moments of clarity that I began to piece together fragments of what had happened. I learned that I had been in a coma for about ten days, that I had undergone surgery, and that I might never walk again. Yet, none of these revelations shook me. Deep within, I just knew: *Everything is going to be okay.*

Amid all the chaos, this calm anchored me. It wasn't the naive hope that everything would return to normal, nor was it denial of the gravity of my situation. It was something deeper; a quiet certainty, an unshakable truth whispering within me: *You're still here. And that is enough.*

It wasn't happiness nor sadness, it was peace, serene and absolute.

I had no idea how long I would remain in that hospital bed. I didn't know what challenges awaited me or how my life would change, but I felt no need to rush toward answers. Somehow, I believed that whatever was to come, I would face it. This peace, a gift in the midst of uncertainty, gave me the strength to just be in the moment; to breathe, to accept, and to trust that everything was going to be okay.

Reflection and Lessons to Consider

- Healing is not only about physical treatment but also about trusting and surrendering to the process.

- A different kind of strength can be found in letting go. It takes courage to hold on, but it takes even greater strength to let go and trust the journey.

- Peace doesn't have to come from knowing all the answers, but it can come from accepting that, at this very moment, being present is enough. In embracing the unknown and resting in a sense of peace, we can find the strength to move forward.

- The power of presence cannot be underestimated. In times of crisis, the quiet, reassuring presence of others can have some healing impact. Being with someone, without needing to say anything, can provide a sense of calm and stability that words alone cannot convey. The act of simply being there for someone, in stillness and understanding, can help them find peace.

- Just as I found peace in that hospital bed, calm can be found in the chaos of life. Trust in the process, surrender when needed, and be present. You are stronger than you think, and peace is always within reach.

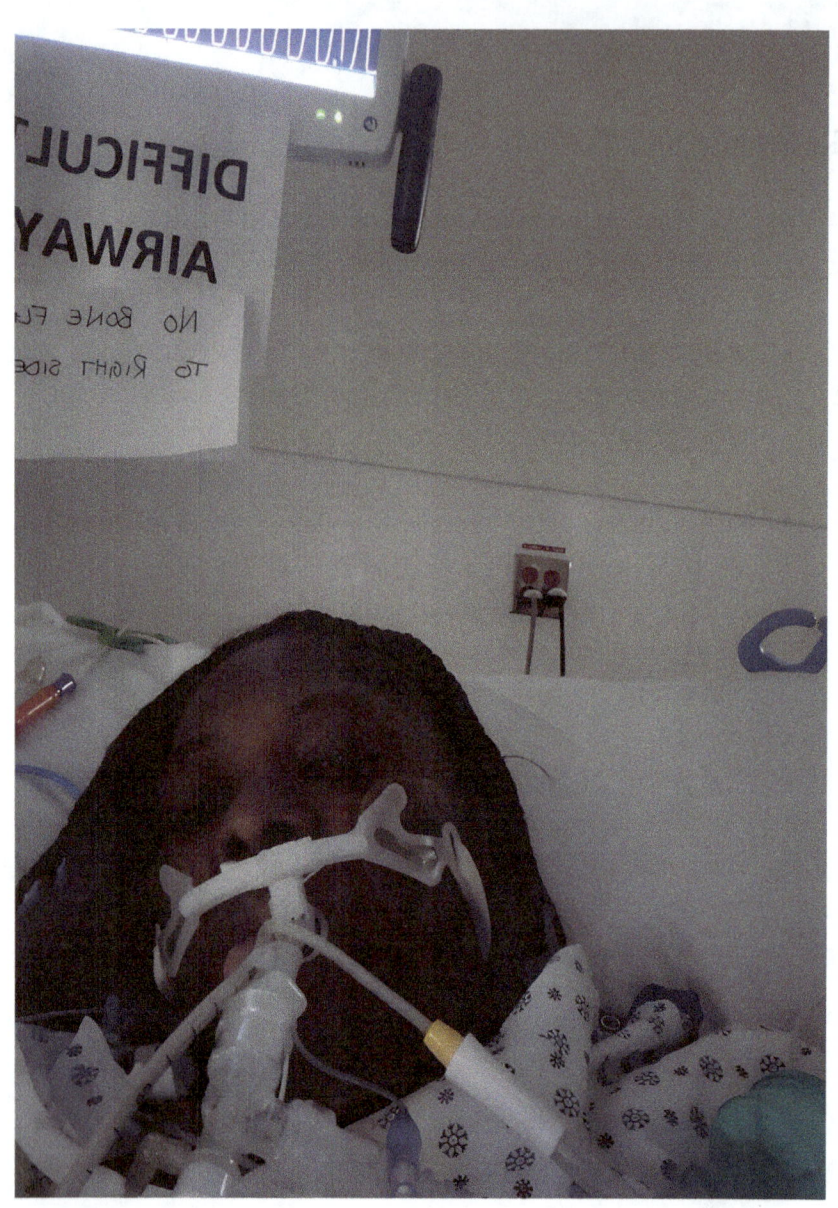

The Bridge We Build

In halls where whispers echo low,
And quiet footsteps softly go,
A hand is held, a voice is kind
A trust begins, both brave and blind.

White coats don't heal, nor stethoscopes,
But hearts aligned with human hopes.
A patient waits, unsure, afraid,
A healer comes, the fear will fade.

With every chart, with every glance,
There lies the chance to take a stance
Not just in science, skill, or speed,
But in the way we truly see the need.

To listen close, to speak with care,
To show the patient, *I am there*.
No masks, no walls, just eye to eye,
Two people, grounded, reaching high.

For healing lives in more than touch,
It lives in faith, in giving much.
It grows when doubt is met with grace,
And trust finds home in time and space.

Here's to those who serve and guide,
With steady hands and hearts wide-eyed.
Each moment shared; each truth discussed
This is the power found in trust.

Chapter 4:

The Dance Between Reality and Delusion

A Vivid Dream or a Delusion?

It was so real. I could feel the steering wheel beneath my fingers, see the familiar streets of home as I drove through them, and heard my son's voice. I was convinced I had gone home, found my son alone, and driven him back to the hospital. It all made perfect sense in my mind. How could I have left him on his own? Of course, I needed to go and get him. Of course, I needed to bring him back with me. I assumed my two older children had gone to their friends; I knew they could take care of themselves; that didn't bother me. But when it comes to Victor, my apprehension was natural, after all, he was too little to manage everything by himself

When we arrived at the hospital, I told Victor to wait in the car. I didn't want the nurses to know I had left. I walked back into my hospital room, reattached the machines to my body, and even intubated myself. I remember feeling triumphant, like I had outsmarted everyone. How clever I was to have snuck out and returned without anyone noticing.

Confession on Paper

The delusion was so convincing that when the nurse came into my room, I gestured for a writing pad. Since I still couldn't speak due to the tube in my throat, I needed a way to communicate. The nurse put my bed in fowler's position, handed me a large yellow pad and a blue pen.

I began writing, confessing my little adventure. I apologized for sneaking out, explained why I had left, and asked the nurse to check on Victor; he was still waiting for me in the parking lot. I was so sure of what I had done that I didn't even question it. The nurse looked at what I had written, her eyes widening slightly, but she didn't argue.

Instead, she calmly asked if it would be okay to call my husband to see if he knew where Victor was. I nodded in relief. Yes, call him, I thought. I needed to make sure my son was safe.

She made the call while I watched from my bed, still certain that my son was out there, waiting for me. I couldn't hear the conversation, but when she hung up, she smiled and told me that Victor was home, safe and sound.

A wave of relief washed over me. I didn't care how Victor had gotten home. I finally allowed myself to relax, closing my eyes and drifting back into sleep.

Wait—That's Impossible

It wasn't until much later, when my mind began to clear, that I realized how impossible it all was. There was no way I could have removed the intubation tube myself. Also, I was paralyzed from the waist down at the time, walking out of the hospital was simply not possible. And yet, my mind had convinced me that it had all happened. It all felt so real.

The Kindness of the Nurse

Looking back, I realize how fortunate I was to have a nurse who understood the fragility of the human mind in moments of trauma. She didn't argue with me or try to convince me that my story wasn't true. She simply went along with it, allowing me to work through my delusion in my own time.

Had she challenged me, had she argued or tried to force reality on me, I might have panicked. I might have tried to prove my story was true by pulling at the tubes or attempting to stand, actions that could have put me in danger. But she didn't push. She didn't make me feel foolish or irrational. Instead, she showed patience, understanding, and a gentle kind of compassion that allowed me to slowly reorient myself to reality. I can never forget her kind gesture toward me. In that time, I needed it the most.

In nursing school, we were taught not to argue with a patient experiencing delusions. It's their reality, and arguing only creates more confusion and distress. But it wasn't until I found myself on the other side, as the delusional patient, not the nurse, that I truly understood the wisdom of that approach.

I don't remember the nurse's name, but I will never forget her kindness. She became one of the many people who helped guide me back to reality, not with force or argument, but with patience and compassion.

A Lesson in Perspective

This experience with delusion taught me an invaluable lesson, one that I've carried with me ever since. Our realities, no matter how strange or far-fetched they may seem to others, are deeply personal. What is real to one person may not align with someone else's version of reality, but that doesn't make it any less valid at the moment.

For me, this was a powerful reminder to approach people with empathy, to understand that their perspective, no matter how different from mine, is still their truth. It's easy to dismiss or judge someone's experience if it doesn't fit within the framework of our own understanding, but the human mind is complex, and sometimes the lines between reality and imagination blur in ways we can't explain.

After this experience, I became more patient with people, more willing to listen and try to understand their reality rather than imposing my own onto them. Whether it's in a medical setting, a personal relationship, or a simple conversation with a stranger, I've learned that empathy and patience can bridge the gap between different perspectives.

The Fragility of the Human Mind

Being in that hospital, caught between reality and delusion, gave me a profound understanding of the fragility of the human mind. I had always thought of myself as strong; mentally, emotionally, physically. I had prided myself on my ability to handle stress and to navigate difficult situations with clarity and reason. But in those moments of confusion, I saw just how vulnerable we all are.

The mind, like the body, can be pushed to its limits. And just as the body sometimes needs time to heal, so too does the mind. My brain had been through trauma, and it was trying to make sense of a reality that didn't align with what it knew. The delusions, as unsettling as they were, were my brain's way of coping, of protecting me from the full weight of what had happened.

Reality Returns, Slowly

As the days passed, my mind began to clear. The delusions became less frequent, and I started to understand more about what had happened to me. I learned about the surgery, about the decisions my family had to make while I was unconscious, and about the long road to recovery that lay ahead. With each passing day, reality became more solid, and the fog of confusion lifted little by little. But one thing still surprises me, I did not panic. I was not afraid of my situation then or what the future looked like. I knew, without a doubt, that everything was going to be okay.

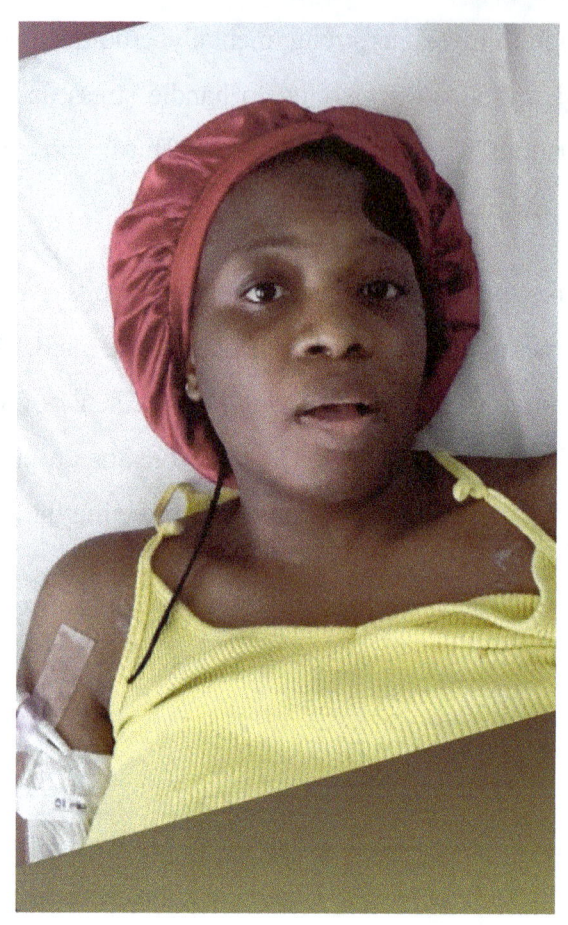

Reflection and Lessons to Consider

- How often do you rush to "fix" your feelings or those of others? What if, instead, you allowed space for confusion, without judgment or the pressure to understand it immediately?

- How do you respond when someone shares a perspective that seems impossible or far-fetched to you? Can you practice patience, knowing that their truth is valid for them, even if it doesn't make sense to you?

- Healing—whether mental, emotional, or physical—isn't a linear journey. It takes time. Sometimes, it's okay to not have clarity. Trust that, in time, answers will come. The key is to remain open, patient, and compassionate throughout the process.

To the Nurse that Cares

She came with kindness in stride,
No judgment, no hurry, just warmth in her eyes.
She is a nurse with so much care in her heart
"I'm here," she whispered, "and I won't let go."

No sharp correction, no harsh reply,
Just gentle truth wrapped in a sigh.
A cooling cloth, a song, a prayer,
A steady heart willing to care.

The patient wept, then smiled a bit,
Her world still foggy, but candles lit.
For even in delusion's cold, dark maze,
The nurse had found a way to raise

A hope, a light, a bridge of grace,
A soft, safe touch in a trembling place.
And though the mind may wander and roam,
With love like that, she wasn't alone.

Chapter 5:

Piercing the Story Together

As the fog of confusion continues to lift, a haunting question took root in my mind: What really happened to me? I could feel the weight of my own body in ways that felt foreign. I was unable to move like I used to. The tube in my throat, though essential, felt like an invader. The concern in the eyes of the nurses and doctors added to my unease. I had collapsed; that much was clear, but what had led me here? And why did it feel like life as I knew it had unraveled?

It wasn't until my husband placed my phone in my hands that reality began to take shape. The screen was flooded with missed calls, messages filled with desperation, prayers, and questions from friends and family. I scrolled through them, trying to comprehend the depth of their worry. How long had I been out of contact? What had happened to me that had shaken so many lives? I was lost in deep thought.

The First Piece of the Puzzle: My Family's Fear

My husband encouraged me to reach out, especially to my family back home in Nigeria. They had been waiting, praying, fearing the worst. I sent short messages, reassurances that I was alive, but it wasn't enough. They needed more. They needed to see my face and hear my voice. Their concern was valid.

With the intubation tube preventing speech, we settled on a video call. When my family saw me, a wave of peace washed over them, their relief was palpable. My mother wept relentlessly. My siblings, who had spent sleepless nights praying for a miracle, clung to my image on the screen. The weight of their emotions stirred something in me. This was not a minor health scare. This had been a battle for my life. And as I regained my consciousness, I realized my life was a precious gift from God.

A Slow Return to Reality

Piece by piece, the story unfolded, not through my memory, but through the voices of those who had lived it for me. My husband recounted the desperate phone call from my coworker, the frantic rush to the hospital, and the doctors' swift decision to transfer me by air ambulance to a specialized facility.

I had been unconscious for ten days. My family had been told the unthinkable—that I might not survive. And if I did, I could be paralyzed. Permanently!

I listened, numb, as they described the urgency of the life-saving surgery, a high-stakes procedure in which doctors had to remove part of my skull to relieve the mounting pressure in my brain. I heard about how my brother, Yemi, had to distance himself from the medical jargon. At some point, he simply told my husband: "Just tell me if she's still breathing please, nothing else."

Against all odds, I had survived. My family rejoiced when they heard I had regained consciousness. But none of us yet knew the truth— I was paralyzed from the waist down.

The Day I Learned the Truth

At first, I didn't realize it. My mind was sharp and clear. I was still me. So, when lunchtime arrived, I made a simple request: I wanted to sit up.

The nurse hesitated. Her eyes revealed her concern, but she didn't argue. I was insistent. I needed to feel normal again. With the help of another nurse, they carefully placed me in a sling and transferred me to a chair beside the bed.

For a brief moment, I felt victorious. Sitting upright felt like reclaiming a piece of myself. But the victory was short-lived. Within minutes, an exhaustion unlike anything I had ever known crashed over me. My arms grew heavy, my breath shallow. I barely lasted five minutes.

I whispered, "Please… I need to go back to bed."

The nurse said nothing, but her expression held volumes. She had known. She had known this moment would come. And yet, there was no judgment, only care.

That was the day I realized I couldn't walk.

A Flame That Would Not Go Out

One might think this truth would shatter me. And yes, it hit hard. But deep inside me, something refused to be extinguished. A quiet, unshakable belief whispered: This is not the end.

I was not broken. I was not defeated. I had survived the impossible. I would walk again.

The doctors gave their prognosis, and the nurses offered their cautious encouragement, but I didn't need anyone to tell me what I already knew in my bones. I would rise, step by step, no matter how long it took.

I did not know then how long this journey would be. I did not know the battles that still lay ahead. But I did know one thing with absolute certainty:

Hope is stronger than fear. And sometimes, the hardest realizations plant the strongest seeds of belief.

Reflection and Lessons to Consider

- Sometimes life brings us to our knees without warning. Sometimes the road we thought we knew disappears beneath our feet. But even when everything seems lost, there is something deep inside that cannot be taken — the will to live, the power to hope, and the courage to believe in better days.

- We are stronger than we know.
  We are braver than we feel.
  And when we lean on faith, family, and the fight within us, even the darkest nights can lead to a beautiful morning.

When the Light Returned

I woke in a room of soft, humming sound,
With whispers and faces gently gathered 'round.
The world was a blur, like a half-remembered dream,
Floating between silence and a distant machine.

Eyes opened slow, heavy like stone,
Body so still, yet I didn't feel alone.
A hand in mine; warm, steady, kind,
Love wrapped around me, easing my mind.

They said I had fallen, deep into night,
A battle was waged, unseen, out of sight.
Two weeks gone, asleep without will,
My body had trembled, but my soul stayed still.

"God kept you," they said with a tear in their eyes,
"You fought with the angels, and you didn't die."
I listened, unsure, with a heart full of awe,
At the strength within me I never once saw.

Alive, awakened, chosen, blessed.
Though broken in body, my spirit stood tall,
For I had been cradled through the darkest fall.
And now with new eyes, I begin again,
With faith in my steps and strength without end.

Let the healing be sure
For I've walked through the fire, and I will endure.
From the edge of goodbye, I've returned with a vow
To live every heartbeat with purpose now.

Chapter 6:

A Glimmer of Hope

The next morning, a couple of doctors appeared at my bedside. Their presence felt different, less clinical and more deliberate as if they carried the news that mattered beyond routine check-ins and sterile medical charts. One of them smiled gently, the kind of smile that tries to bridge the gap between professional detachment and genuine care.

"We're going to transfer you to the Neuro Unit as soon as a bed becomes available. This is in the hopes that you'll eventually be moved to the Rehabilitation Unit, but that will depend on how you do on the Neuro Unit," one of them said, his voice steady, almost casual.

But the words that hit me like a lightning bolt were **Rehabilitation Unit.**

For a moment, everything else faded; the rhythmic beeping of the monitors, the sterile scent of disinfectant that clung to the air, the faint murmurs of footsteps and hushed voices from the hallway. None of it mattered. My heart swelled with a quiet, powerful hope. **Rehabilitation.** That word was more than just part of a medical plan, it was a promise. A whisper of possibility. It echoed in my mind like a sacred mantra: They believe I might be able to walk again.

I didn't say much. I nodded politely, trying to maintain the calm expression of someone who understood. But inside, my thoughts raced in a thousand directions, tangled with emotions I couldn't quite name. *Did they hear about yesterday?* I wondered. *Did they know how I had insisted on getting out of bed, determined to sit in that chair even when my body protested? Was that why they believed in me now?*

But I didn't ask. I didn't need to. Their words were enough.

A Quiet Transfer in the Night

I don't remember exactly how many days passed between that conversation and the actual transfer. Time lost its meaning when my routine was stitched together by the same sounds, the same ceiling, the same rhythm of day and night blending into one.

But this I remember: it was the middle of the night. The hospital was quieter than usual, the kind of silence that feels both peaceful and heavy. Two people appeared at my bedside with a stretcher, their presence shadowed by the dim hallway lights. My night nurse was with them, her voice soft as she leaned over and said, "There's a bed available in the Neuro Unit. We're transferring you now."

Everything happened in the blink of an eye. The coldness of the stretcher seeped through the thin sheets as they moved me, and the fluorescent lights overhead flickered past like snapshots of this new chapter unfolding. I stared at the ceiling, letting the motion soothe me, even though I wasn't entirely sure what I was feeling—hope, fear, anticipation, maybe all of them woven together.

When we arrived at the Neuro Unit, the difference was immediate. It felt dated, worn from years of stories like mine etched into its walls. It was nothing like the ICU, where the technology hummed with life, and every surface gleamed with sterile precision. The Neuro Unit felt older and quieter in a different way, less about survival and more about endurance.

I was still trying to process my new surroundings when, not long after settling in, two more hospital workers appeared with another stretcher. "We're moving you to another room," they said. I didn't ask why. At that point, I had learned to surrender to the flow of hospital life, where plans changed with little explanation.

This time, I was moved to a shared room, a curtain stretched between two beds to mark the boundary between strangers turned roommates. On one side, me. On the other, a man whose name I didn't know, whose face I hadn't seen yet. He was snoring as I was wheeled in.

I didn't know what tomorrow would bring. But I knew this: every move, every room, every small shift was part of the journey. And even though I wasn't walking yet, with every step taken for me, I was still moving forward.

A Knowing Beyond Faith

I have often wondered where my faith came from because, through the doctors' poor prognosis, my faith never wavered. But now, I'm not even sure if I should call it faith. It was more than that. It was a knowing. A deep, unwavering certainty. I just knew I would walk again. There was not a single doubt in my mind.

In my heart, I was already standing tall.

Reclaiming Control

Ever since I became conscious and the breathing tubes removed, one thought nagged at me constantly, as persistent as the beeping monitors and the sterile smell of antiseptic that filled my hospital room: I wanted this catheter out.

It felt like a chain, an invisible shackle tethering me not just to the bed but to a version of myself that felt powerless. Every nurse who entered my room became an unwitting target of my polite but desperate plea. "Can you please remove the catheter?" I'd ask over and over. And every time, I got the same answer, spoken gently but firmly: "Not yet."

I understood why. It was because of my paralysis from the waist down. But understanding didn't make it easier.

One morning, I asked for something different. "Could I get an empty syringe?" I said casually. To my surprise, the nurse handed it to me without hesitation. That was all I needed.

I waited patiently for her to leave. Then, my steady, practiced hands deflated the balloon holding the catheter in place—freedom!

But the victory was short-lived. Minutes later, I felt the overwhelming urge to pee. I pressed the call bell. No one came. Reality crashed over me: I couldn't stand.

By the time a nurse arrived, my discarded catheter lay beside the bed, a symbol of my impulsive rebellion. Her expression shifted; disbelief, mild annoyance, but beneath it all, a flicker of understanding. She sighed and called for assistance. Moments later, someone arrived with incontinence briefs—attends, as they called them.

Before leaving, the nurse paused. She pointed to the side of my head where a piece of my skull—a bone flap—was missing. "Be careful," she said quietly. "You don't have any protection on that side of your head."

Her words hung in the air. Not just as a physical warning, but as something deeper, a reminder that while my spirit was strong, my body was still fragile.

And yet, despite the mess I'd made, despite the discomfort and the nurse's unimpressed sighs, I felt something powerful: I had taken back some control.

And that day, lying in that hospital bed, I might have been paralyzed, vulnerable, and covered in attends, but in my heart, I was free.

Reflection and Lessons to Consider

- Can you look at your own challenges and find the quiet belief that no matter what happens, you too can rise—one step at a time?

- Strength lies in the will to rise again. Your circumstances don't define your strength. It's the will to keep going, even when things are tough, that makes you resilient. It's okay to take small steps, knowing that each one is progress.

A Glimmer of Hope

In the shadow of sorrow, when the night feels long,
When nothing feels right, and everything's wrong,
A whisper breaks through like a soft-spoken song
A glimmer of hope, so gentle, yet strong.

It flickers like stars on a storm-covered sky,
A promise that pain will soon pass by.
Not loud, not bold, but steady and true,
A quiet reminder: you'll make it through.

It lives in the dawn after cold, restless sleep,
In prayers you once mumbled, now buried deep.
It hides in a smile, in the eyes of a friend,
In the start of a letter you forgot to send.

Hope doesn't shout, it simply stays near,
Wiping one tear, then the next tear.
It's the breath you take when you thought you could not,
The step you still take when courage feels shot.

Hold on, dear heart, though the journey feels steep,
There's strength in your soul that the world cannot keep.
That glimmer will grow, just give it the space,
And soon you'll be walking in God's healing grace.

Chapter 7:

The Night My Foot Remembered

The Neuro team stopped by my bedside every morning like clockwork, a small crowd of white coats, stethoscopes slung around their necks, faces half-etched with curiosity, half-masked in professional detachment. Their routine was always the same: polite greetings, careful observations, and then the tests. They poked, prodded, and pressed, searching for any sign of life in my lower extremities, any flicker of sensation, any twitch of movement.

But every day felt like a rerun of the one before.

"Can you feel this?"

No.

"Try to move your toes."

Nothing.

The disappointment settled over me like a second blanket; one I couldn't throw off. But I held onto that one thing they couldn't measure with their tests: *hope.*

I had been told that I needed to show some improvement before I could be transferred to the Rehabilitation Unit. That word—*rehabilitation*—had become my lighthouse, guiding me through the fog of hospital routines and sterile walls. But day after day, my body remained stubbornly silent.

But nights were different.

Nights were mine. In the quiet darkness, when the hospital settled into a hushed rhythm of beeping monitors and distant footsteps, I waged my own private battle. While others slept, I stayed awake, willing my legs to remember. *Move,* I'd whisper in my mind, *just move.* I'd stare at my feet until my eyes blurred, concentrating so hard it felt like I could bend reality if I just believed enough.

But nothing happened. Night after night, my legs remained still, indifferent to my silent pleas.

Until one night.

It was like any other—dim lights casting long shadows across the room, the distant hum of machines, the loud snores of my roommate. But this time, as I focused with everything I had, something shifted. A flicker. A tremor. *My foot moved.*

It wasn't much; a small twitch, barely noticeable, but to me, it was a miracle. My heart raced. I felt like the entire universe had paused to witness this quiet rebellion of my body against paralysis. *It moved,* I kept repeating in my head, over and over, afraid the memory might slip away like a dream if I didn't hold onto it tightly enough.

I could barely sleep after that. I couldn't wait to show the doctors during their morning rounds.

When they arrived, I was practically vibrating with excitement. "Watch this," I said eagerly. I stared at my foot, willing it to move again. I concentrated and begged silently, but nothing happened.

Nothing.

My foot refused to cooperate as if it had retreated into hiding, leaving me with nothing but my words. "It moved last night," I insisted, my voice tinged with desperation and a flicker of doubt.

The doctors smiled politely, nodding in the way people do when they are not sure if they believe you but don't want to be unkind. Then they left, their footsteps fading down the hall, taking my excitement with them.

But I didn't let that moment define me.

If my foot had moved once, it could move again. *I knew it.*

So, I practiced. Day and night. I stared at my legs, focused until my head ached, whispered silent commands to muscles that had forgotten how to listen. Slowly, something began to change. The movements were no longer fleeting accidents; they became deliberate, controlled, *mine.*

I could move my legs. Not perfectly, not with ease, but enough.

The next time the doctors came, I didn't just tell them, I showed them. I lifted a foot, small but undeniable, proof etched in the movement itself. I watched their eyes shift from polite indifference to surprise, their professional masks cracking just enough for me to see it: *belief.*

Shortly after that, I was transferred to the Rehabilitation Unit.

But this story isn't just about the moment my foot moved. It's about everything that led up to it; the countless nights of failure, the quiet battles fought when no one was watching, the unshakeable belief that even when nothing seemed to change, *something* was happening beneath the surface.

Sometimes, progress whispers before it roars.

And on that night, in the dark, when the world was asleep, my foot whispered back.

Reflection and Lessons to Consider

- Healing — whether it's physical, mental, or emotional — is not a race. It's a journey. Be patient with yourself. Give it time. Hold on to hope, and never give up

- What if the real victory lies not in how fast we can fix ourselves, but in the courage to keep trying, even when progress feels invisible? Each small attempt, each breath, each flicker of movement, is part of the greater process. Healing demands patience, self-compassion, and persistence.

- Have you ever measured your progress based on what others can see, only to feel discouraged when your growth isn't obvious to them? What if the most important steps are the ones you take when no one is looking?

- There's no set timeline for healing, and there's no perfect path. Some days will be slow, and progress might seem invisible. But even the smallest step is a step forward.

- Trust in the process. Sometimes, healing is happening beneath the surface before it's visible. Relax, let your body and mind work together. The journey is as important as the destination.

Healing Is Not Perfection

You don't need to rise like nothing is wrong,
Or wear a smile and act so strong.
You don't need plans or perfect pace
You just need time, and a little grace.

Some days will feel like moving slow,
Like progress hides or doesn't show.
But every breath, each small try,
Is proof you're healing, by and by.

It's not a race or flawless climb,
But steady steps through patient time.
Some wins are quiet, hard to see
Like choosing rest, or letting be.

You may feel tired, you may feel weak,
But strength shows up in moments bleak.
In choosing hope when skies are grey,
In getting up each brand-new day.

There may be pain, there may be fear,
But healing means you're still right here.
Not perfect - no one ever is-
But present, trying, and that's what this is.

Take it slow, and don't lose sight:
The smallest steps still lead to light.
Perfection's never been the goal
Persistence, love, and healing whole.

Chapter 8:

The Rehabilitation Unit

The *Rehabilitation Unit*—the name spoke for itself. This was where people came to fight their way back to life, surrounded by an army of specialists: neurologists, physiotherapists, physiatrists, neurosurgeons. Each of them carried expertise, knowledge, and clinical precision, but none of them carried what I held within me—*an unshakable will to recover.*

For the first few days, I observed everything around me; the structured schedules, the therapy sessions, and the careful monitoring of every small change in my condition. I had imagined that being on the Rehabilitation Unit would feel like being on the fast track to recovery, but the reality hit differently. Progress here wasn't loud or dramatic. It was slow, almost painstaking, measured in tiny, incremental victories that often felt invisible.

During one of the doctors' morning rounds, I couldn't hold back. "Based on your experience," I asked, trying to mask the desperation in my voice, "how long do you think I'll be here?"

The doctor paused, his expression thoughtful but guarded, as if carefully choosing words that wouldn't crush me. "At least six months," he said gently.

Six months?

The words hit me like a punch to the chest. I tried to process it, but it sat heavy in my heart. *Six more months* in this sterile environment, confined by hospital walls, with the constant buzz of machines and the suffocating routine of dependency. I still couldn't stand on my own, but my spirit was restless. My mind refused to accept that timeline.

Steps of Defiance

Just two days after hearing that news, fueled by frustration and stubborn defiance, I decided I was done waiting. I didn't call for help. I didn't think about the warnings or the risks. I simply *tried.*

I attempted to get out of bed by myself.

It didn't go well.

I ended up on the floor, tangled in sheets and disappointment. The fall wasn't graceful, it was a harsh, it was a reminder of the reality that my mind had not come to terms with. Within moments, nurses rushed in, their faces painted with frustration and fear.

They weren't just angry. They were furious!

"You could've seriously hurt yourself," one of them scolded, her voice sharp with a mix of professional concern and personal exasperation. "You don't have protection on that side of your head. Do you understand how dangerous that is?"

I did. I understood completely. The missing piece of my skull, still yet to be replaced after cranial surgery, was more than just a medical fact, it was a fragile reality I had recklessly ignored.

I was deeply apologetic, not just for the trouble I'd caused but for the fear I saw in their eyes. They weren't just upset, they cared. That realization settled into me, softening my pride just enough to let gratitude in.

But even in that moment of regret, there was something else beneath the surface: a flicker of something stubborn and fierce. *At least I tried,* I thought. *At least I didn't just lie there waiting.*

Later that day, someone brought a wheelchair to my bedside.

"This is for you," they said, their tone somewhere between cautious and hopeful. "But, you still need to call for help when you want to move."

I nodded, promising to follow the rules, but inside, my heart swelled with quiet triumph. The wheelchair wasn't just a tool, it was a sign of progress. A symbol that I was no longer entirely confined to the bed. *This was movement. This was freedom, even if it had wheels.*

The structure of my recovery became more defined after that. Every morning, a physiotherapist assistant was sent to my room to help me exercise around the unit. They guided me through stretches, mobility drills, and strength exercises. Simple things on the surface, but monumental when every movement felt like a negotiation between my mind and my body.

Twice a week, I met with physiotherapists for more intense bodywork. These sessions were grueling, pushing me beyond the limits I thought existed. They manipulated my limbs, activated muscles I'd nearly forgotten, and challenged me to find strength buried deep within. It wasn't just physical; it was mental warfare. The pain, the frustration, the slow pace of progress, they all threatened to overshadow the small victories.

But with every stretch, every assisted step, I grew stronger.

For the next few days, I did as I was instructed. I pressed the call button, waited for help, and allowed the nurses to assist me with transfers. But with every passing day, something grew inside me—*confidence.*

One morning, I didn't call for help. I transferred myself into the wheelchair. I wheeled myself to the bathroom, my hands steady on the wheels, my heart racing with exhilaration. It was a small act of rebellion, but it felt like climbing a mountain.

Then one day, I decided to push the boundary even further.

Instead of using the wheelchair, I stood—unsteady but determined—and reached for the wall. I held onto it, using it as my anchor, inching my way to the bathroom with shaky steps and sheer willpower.

When the staff noticed, they were both surprised and impressed. They didn't scold me this time. They *noticed* the progress. Shortly after, they brought me a walker.

It felt like leveling up.

The walker gave me more stability, but even that wasn't enough for me. I wasn't satisfied with just "getting by." I wanted *more.* I wanted to feel my own strength, not rely on frames and devices.

So, after a while, I left the walker behind. They gave me a cane.

And you can probably guess what happened next.

The cane didn't last long. It was a brief companion, a temporary crutch. Because soon after, I started walking on my own. Unsteady, yes. Wobbly, sure. But *walking.*

Every shaky step felt like a declaration: *I am more than my limitations. I am more than my diagnosis. I am more than what anyone expected of me.*

I wasn't just recovering. I was *reclaiming* my life, one determined step at a time.

Reflection and Lessons to Consider

The process of recovery can often feel like a battle between the limitations of the body and the strength of the will. And yet, sometimes, those limitations are what reveal the true power of the spirit—the deep, unyielding belief that there is always more to give, even when the path seems unclear.

- Have you ever felt impatient with the slow pace of your own healing or growth, expecting results to come faster than they do? What would happen if you allowed yourself to trust in the process, knowing that every step—no matter how slow—is part of your progress?

- In the face of setbacks, what would it look like for you to choose persistence, even when the road ahead seems uncertain?

- The journey to healing or achieving anything meaningful often requires not just physical effort, but mental endurance. The frustration of slow progress, the quiet moments when you feel like giving up—those are all part of your growth. Keep going, even when you don't see immediate results.

- Always keep this in mind; you are not defined by your limitations, but by your determination to move beyond them.

- Healing is about the moments when you rise despite the setbacks, when you try again even after falling. Every small victory, every hesitant step, is proof of the strength that lies within you. Can you recognize the progress in the places where it's hardest to see? When you look back, will you be able to see the person you were and the person you've become? How far will you push your own limits today?

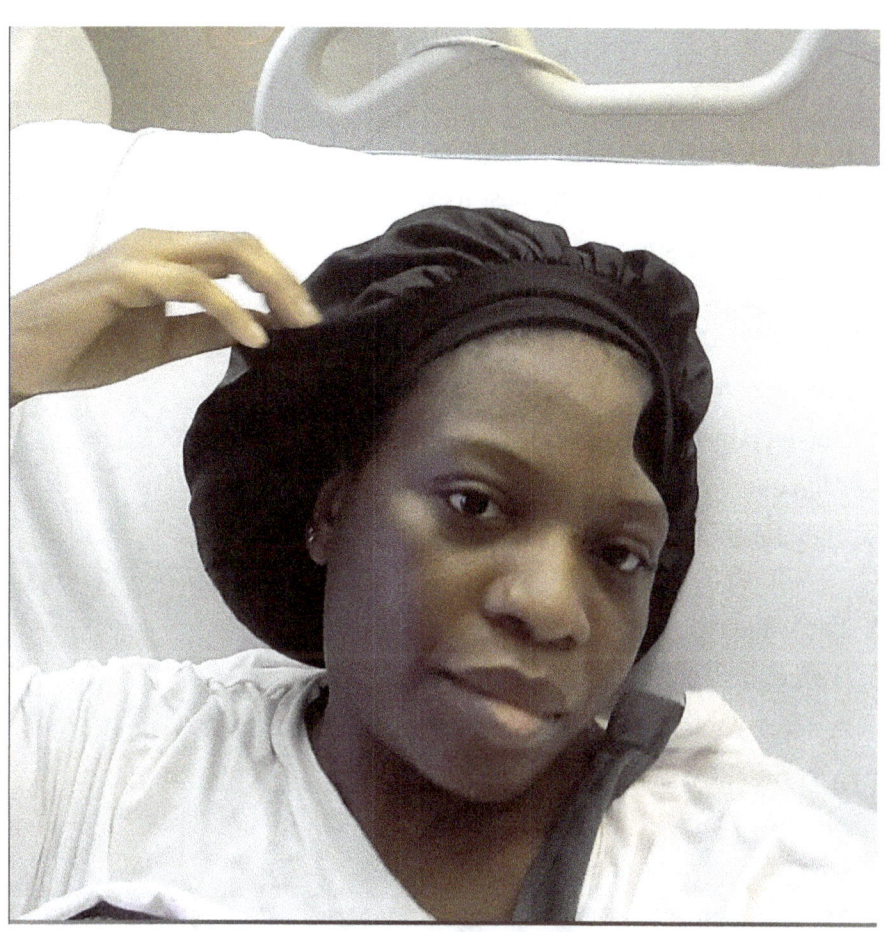

One Step at a Time

In a quiet room, with hope so near,
A soul stands tall, pushing past fear.
Each breath is strong, each day is new,
With one clear thought: *I will pull through.*

The body aches, the journey's slow,
But deep inside, the sparks still glow.
With every lift, with every try,
They reach again, they aim so high.

The walker waits, the floor feels far,
But courage shines like a guiding star.
A nurse says, "You can do this—start."
And strength is born in beating heart.

One step forward, then one more,
Through pain and sweat, through every sore.
But louder still, the fight within.

The mirror shows a warrior's face,
Not one who's lost, but one with grace.
This road is hard, but not the end,
Each day a climb, each hour a friend.

The healing comes, though it feels slow.
You're not alone, you're standing tall
And one day soon… you'll walk it all.

Chapter 9:

The Unstoppable Spirit

Walking Against the Odds

The first steps were shaky, but I didn't sit back, and I continued with my resolute. It wasn't perfect, but that didn't matter. I had no doubt in my head that I would walk perfectly again. It was only a matter of time. The medical team had said, *"At least six months before discharge."* But I knew that wasn't going to be my story. I didn't need to ask. My progress was proof enough.

Barely a month had passed, and I was already moving. My body was catching up to what my mind already knew: I was healing faster than expected. That's when I started asking about the missing piece of my skull.

Too Fast, Too Soon?

At first, the doctors and nurses dismissed my questions. *"You're rushing,"* they said. *"You need time."* But I wasn't interested in waiting.

Then, I got an answer, *"Maybe in two months."*

Two months? Doing what? Sitting in a hospital bed, waiting? That didn't sit well with me. If I was already walking, why couldn't I finish the rest of my recovery at home? I asked again. And again.

I must have asked one too many times because eventually, someone said, *"Well, you could leave… but it would be Against Medical Advice."*

Against Medical Advice. These three words carried immense weight. They meant I could walk out if I wanted, but the responsibility would be mine. There would be no safety net, no structured care, just me, my willpower, and an uncertain road ahead.

For a moment, I considered it. After all, I was already proving them wrong. But then I thought about two things:

1. I still needed the missing part of my skull put back in. That wasn't something I could handle on my own.

2. Leaving Against Medical Advice might affect my disability insurance.

So, I stayed. Not because I wanted to, but because it was the smarter choice. And if there was one thing I had learned, it was that survival wasn't just about pushing forward, it was about knowing *when* to push and *when* to wait.

The Hard Road of Recovery

Staying meant more physio. More rec therapy. Occupational therapy. Speech therapy. Cognitive therapy. Psychological counseling. Vision therapy. The list seemed endless.

But so was my determination.

Every session, every exercise, every challenge, I took them on with one thought in my mind: *I am getting out of here sooner than they think.*

I wasn't just a patient. I was a warrior in a battle against time, against expectations, against anything that said I couldn't. And I was winning.

A New Dawn

Now, as I look back, and I try to connect the dots, I see more than just the hospital stay, I see a journey filled with courage and unwavering spirit. Every doubt, every question, every moment of hesitation was part of a larger story. A story where I learned that healing is not a straight line but a winding road with hills and valleys.

I discovered that true strength comes not from ignoring caution, but from knowing when to push ahead and when to trust the process. I learned to value the wisdom of the past while carving out my own future. The journey ahead might still be long, but with each passing day, I become a little bit stronger, a little bit wiser, and a whole lot more determined.

My story is a reminder that no matter how tough the road, there is always hope on the horizon, a new dawn is waiting just around the corner.

Reflection and Lessons to Consider

- How do you balance your own desires for progress with the need to respect your limits and the process of healing or growth?

- When you set out to achieve something—whether it's healing, personal growth, or overcoming a challenge— expect the unexpected. Sometimes, the path you imagine won't be the one you walk, but it will still take you exactly where you need to go. Trust the process. Trust yourself.

- What if the road to your goals wasn't about getting to the destination quickly, but about what you learn along the way? Can you embrace the small victories, the moments of uncertainty, and the lessons in patience? What will it take for you to trust that the road you're on, however winding, will lead you to where you're meant to be?

An Unstoppable Spirit

You can't break what's built to rise,
Like stars that burn in darkest skies.
A heart that's strong, a will that's true
There's nothing it can't walk through.

Storms may come and winds may roar,
But still, it stands.
Not out of pride, or stubborn fight,
But fueled by faith and inner light.

It falls, it stumbles, it may cry,
But never quits, and always tries.
Each setback just becomes a tool
To shape a soul that won't be fooled.

It keeps on going, step by step,
With dreams to chase and promises kept.
So if you're tired, but holding tight,
You are the fire, you are the fight.

Remember this when days feel tough:
You were made from the strongest stuff.
No wall too high, no path too steep
An unstoppable spirit does not sleep.

Chapter 10:

A Bittersweet Reunion

One day, my husband brought our children for a visit. When Victoria, then 12 years old, saw me, she burst into tears. It broke her heart to see her mom in such a state. Yet, between her tears, she whispered words of gratitude—that I still remembered their names and all the happy moments we had shared together. I know she had seen movies where characters lose their memories after a brain injury, and she worried that I might forget who I truly was. In that moment, her concern and love filled the room with both sorrow and hope.

See, before everything unfolded, Victoria once told me about a strange dream she had. In her dream, my head looked dented. I brushed it off at the time, saying it was just a dream. But that day, when my children visited me at the hospital, my daughter's eyes filled with both sadness and wonder. As she saw me, she softly said, "Mummy, this is how your head looked in the dream I had." Her words stirred something deep within me—a mix of pain and a strange comfort that somehow this dream had foretold a piece of my journey.

Fuel for a New Beginning

After their visit, I felt a spark of hope that pushed me toward discharge. I longed to be home, to feel the warmth of my family, and to rebuild my life outside the hospital walls. My mind was racing with questions about when my missing skull piece would be fixed, and the promise of a new chapter urged me to ask for answers once more.

The Family Meeting That Changed Everything

Soon, my medical team suggested a family meeting. There, my husband, the doctors, the therapists, and I sat together to talk about my progress and my concerns. During that meeting, they set a date—a few days away—for when my skull would be reattached, and they promised that my discharge was not far off. The joy I felt on that day was hard to describe. It wasn't just relief; it was the overwhelming excitement of a new beginning, a second chance at life.

A Weekend of Freedom

I had one more wish: to go home for the weekend before my second surgery. Initially, the request was turned down. But soon after, a kind nurse came to my room with good news. I was granted a brief return home, with the condition that I follow strict COVID protocols and take extra care with my head since it wasn't fixed yet. I promised them I would follow every rule. That weekend, surrounded by my loving family, I felt a deep sense of belonging and renewal. I left the hospital on Saturday, September 3rd, 2022 and returned on Monday, September 5th, 2022, feeling refreshed, recharged, and more determined than ever.

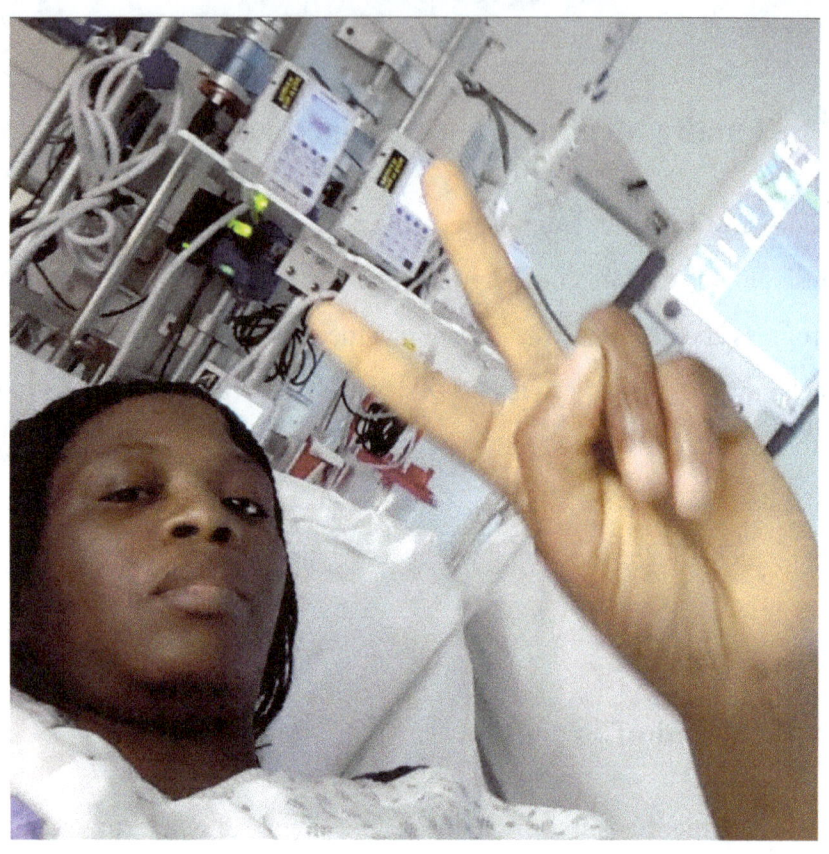

The Leap of Renewal

Then came Wednesday, September 7th, 2022—the day of my second surgery, the day my skull would be restored. I remember being carefully wheeled into the operating room. The medical team introduced themselves and explained what would happen. An oxygen mask was gently placed over my face, and before I knew it, I drifted away into a deep sleep. The next thing I remember is waking up in the recovery room, a bit groggy but still filled with hope. I was then moved to another unit for careful monitoring, and by the next day, I was transferred back to my original unit.

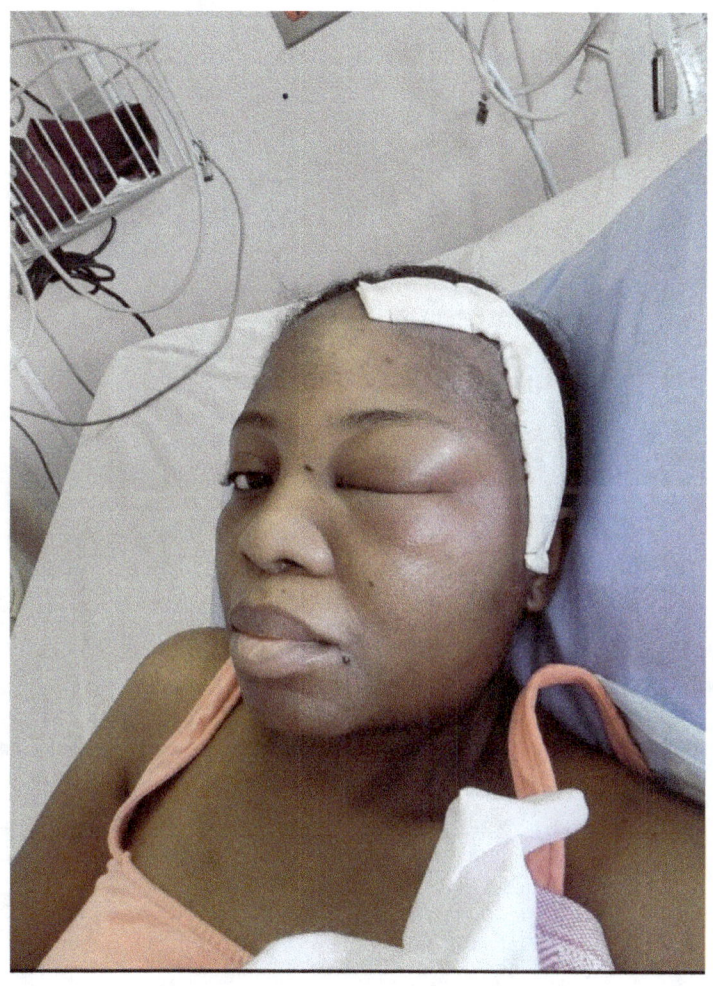

My missing skull restored.

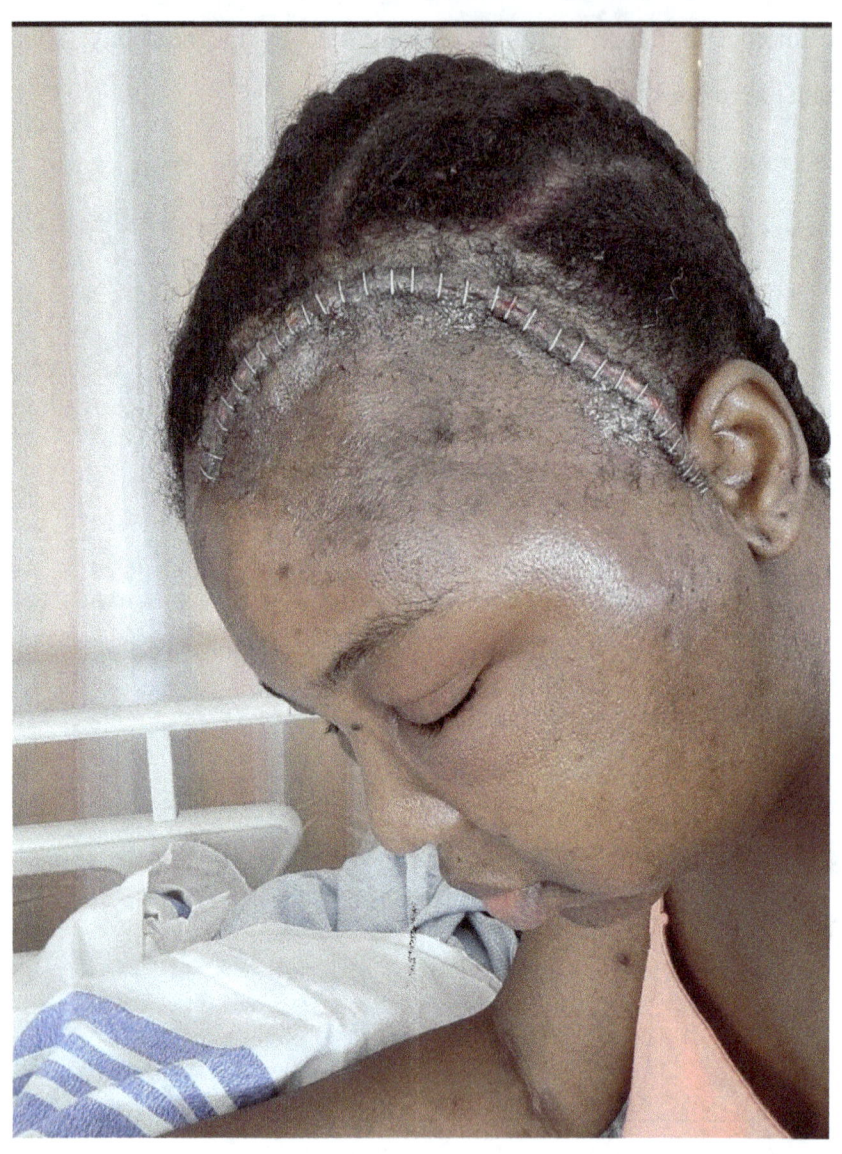

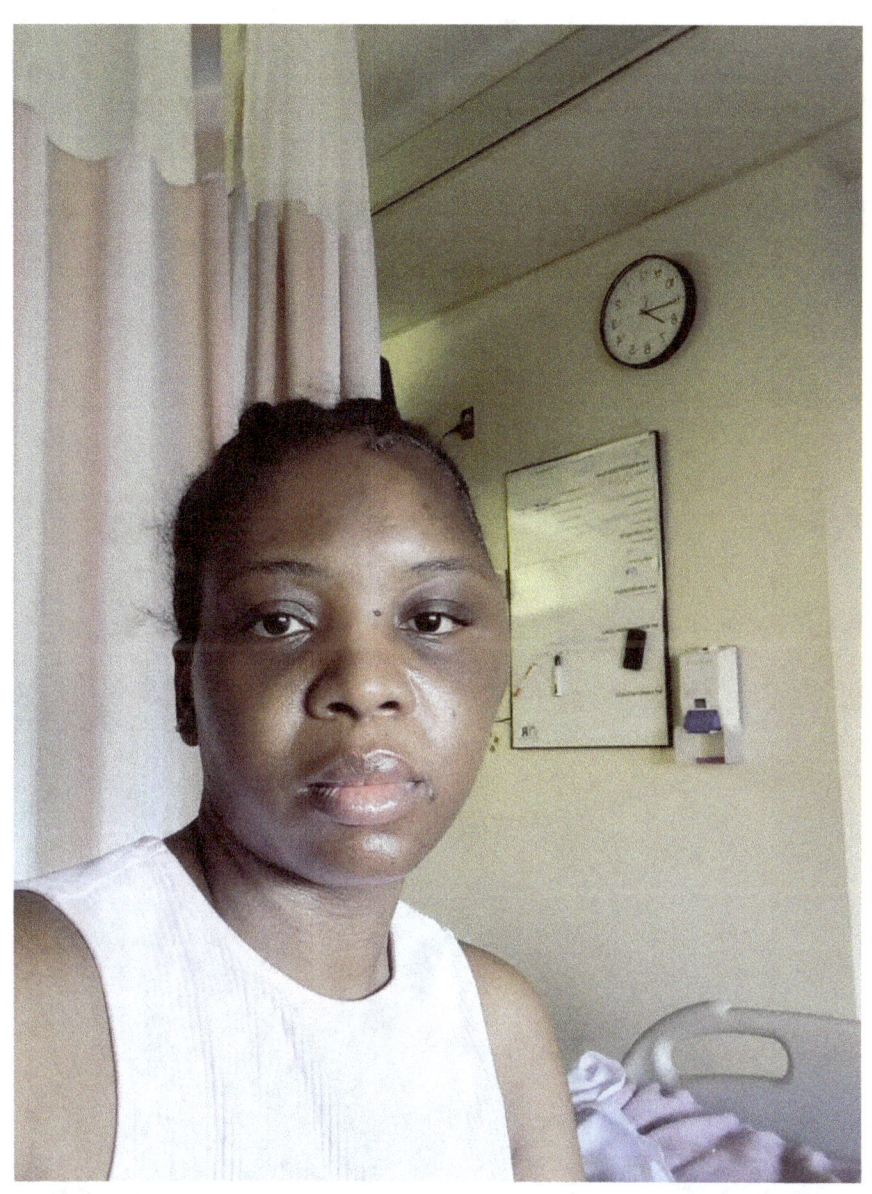

On September 20th, 2022—just **8 weeks and 5 days** after my medical emergency and hospital admission—I was discharged. I didn't leave in a wheelchair. I didn't need any assistance.

I walked out of that hospital on my own two feet!

It was a moment I will never forget. The same place where doctors once doubted if I would ever walk again was now the place where I took my first steps toward freedom. The same halls where I had fought through pain, therapy, and endless challenges were now behind me.

I walked—not just as a patient who had healed but as a survivor who had conquered.

There were moments along the way when the road seemed too hard, when the pain felt unbearable, and when the future was uncertain. But I never gave up. I never accepted limits. I never let fear define my destiny.

This journey has taught me that the mind is powerful, and that even the darkest nights can eventually give way to the dawn.

I walked out of that hospital not just alive, but reborn— wiser, and ready to embrace life like never before.

This is not the end of my story. This is just the beginning.

Beyond the Hospital: A Journey of Strength

Leaving the hospital was not the end of my healing—it was the beginning of a new chapter. The therapies continued, even after my second surgery. The hospital ensured I had a physiotherapist visit me at home, guiding me through exercises that strengthened my body. Twice a week, I logged onto Zoom for therapy sessions, pushing through every challenge with determination.

I kept fighting. Step by step, session by session, I grew stronger—not just physically, but mentally and emotionally too.

And then, after almost 2 long years of recovery, I did something I had dreamed of for years. I traveled to Nigeria—my first visit in 16 years after moving to Canada. It was more than just a trip. It was a homecoming. A moment of reconnection. A powerful reminder of how far I had come.

With some of my family members in Nigeria

From left to right; my brother- Fredrick Aderinto, myself, my sister-in-law Olanike Aderinto, my mother Alice Aderinto, my brother Adeyemi Aderinto, my brother Aderemi Aderinto and my sister-in-law Damilola Aderinto.

With my nieces and nephews in Nigeria

Left to right: my mother Alice Aderinto, myself, my brother Adeyemi
Aderinto and his wife Damilola Aderinto.

My beautiful sister-in-law Olayemi Aderinto came with me to the
airport to bid goodbye as I left Nigeria

With my brother, Adeyemi C. Aderinto.

One of the greatest highlights of my visit to Nigeria was touring my brother, **Adeyemi Aderinto's**, incredible company, **SQI** (https://edu.sqi.ng/). Walking through the different campuses across various states filled me with overwhelming pride. Seeing the impact of his work—the students eager to learn, the classrooms buzzing with innovation, and the vision unfolding before my eyes—was truly inspiring.

As I traveled from campus to campus, I could feel the energy, the passion, and the dedication that fueled **SQI's** mission. It was more than just an educational institution—it was a place of transformation, just like my own journey had been.

That trip was more than a homecoming. It was a full-circle moment. After everything I had been through—months of uncertainty, recovery, and therapies—I was no longer just surviving.

I was **living again.**

Enjoying. Exploring. Embracing life with a heart full of gratitude. Stronger than ever.

From a hospital bed to walking on my own. From uncertainty to strength. From survival to thriving.

This journey has been proof that no matter how hard life knocks you down, you can rise again. Stronger. Wiser. Unstoppable.

Hold On to Hope

When the night feels never-ending,
and the weight is hard to bear,
hold on to hope,
it's still there.

When the silence feels too loud,
and the tears won't seem to dry,
hope is the whisper
that says, "Try."

It doesn't shout.
It doesn't shine.
It's just a light
that waits behind.

It's in a breath
you didn't think you'd take,
in a step
you didn't know you'd make.

Hope is small
but never weak.
It stays alive
when days are bleak.

When your heart feels pulled apart,
and you're too tired to cope,
rest if you must,
but hold on to hope.

Back to Life, Back to Purpose

After everything—the collapse, the recovery, the therapies, the journey back home—I am now back to work, working full-time.

It feels surreal yet powerful. To go from lying in a hospital bed, unsure of the future, to standing tall, fully back in the flow of life. Every day at work is a reminder of how far I've come, of the strength that carried me through, and of the purpose that still drives me forward.

I am not just back to work—I am back to thriving, back to making an impact. Back to living fully and embracing every moment with gratitude.

This journey has taught me that no setback is final. With faith, resilience, and determination, you can rise again, reclaim your life, and emerge stronger than ever.

The Scars I Sustained from My Experience

The scars I carry are more than just marks on my skin—they are proof of the battles I fought and the strength I found within. One of these scars is on my head, where the surgery was done. The area looks a little darker and dented compared to the other side of my head. To some, it might seem like a flaw, but to me, it is a badge of honor. Every time I see it, I remember the fierce fight it took to stand where I am today.

Another scar is hidden in my voice. The intubation left a mark that changed the way I sound. I have often been asked, "What's up with your voice?" and I always end up explaining my story of survival, pain, and an unwavering spirit that kept me going and transformed me into a new person. My voice, though different, is a reminder that every challenge I faced has shaped who I am.

There was one day at the hospital that still lingers in my memory. I had walked up to the front desk to ask for water—a small act made more formal by the COVID protocols in place. Instead of receiving help, the receptionist mimicked my voice back to me, repeating the very question I had asked. In that moment, I felt a sting of insensitivity. It was a reminder that even in places of healing, we can sometimes be met with unexpected hurt.

Yet, I have learned that these scars, both seen and unseen, are symbols of my resilience. They speak of long nights, complex therapies, and the countless moments when I chose hope over despair. I wear them proudly as my badge of honor. They remind me that every setback, every insensitive moment, was just another step on the road to becoming more powerful, more resilient and unbreakable force.

Reflection and Lessons to Consider

- Scars are proof of survival, not defeat.

  We all face challenges, big and small. Sometimes the wounds we carry are visible, but more often, they're hidden within. Our scars are proof that we survived. They remind us that we've fought battles, endured pain, and come out the other side stronger. So, when you look at the scars on your body or in your heart, don't see them as flaws, see them as symbols of your strength, of your ability to keep going, even when the road gets tough.

- Don't be afraid to show your scars, to share your story. There's power in vulnerability; power to inspire others and, most importantly, power to heal yourself.

- Never underestimate the power of belief; believe in your strength, believe in your potential, and believe that you can overcome anything.

- We never know what someone else is going through, and sometimes, the kindness we offer can be a lifeline. So, be gentle with others and with yourself. We're all fighting battles, and a little compassion can go a long way.

The Scar I Sustained

The scar I sustained

is not just skin deep.

It tells a story;

of pain I met,

and strength I found.

This scar is a reminder;

that I survived.

That I kept going

when I had every reason to stop.

When you see it,

don't pity me.

See the fight.

See the will.

See the fire that couldn't be put out.

I earned this scar.

And I'm still standing.

Still healing.

Still rising.

A Heart Full of Gratitude

As I reflect on this journey, one truth echoes louder than the rest: I did not walk this path alone. Every step forward was carried by the strength, love, and selflessness of others. This book would not exist without them.

To **Chiki Vegter**—you left the comfort of your home and came into mine, caring for my children until my husband could return. Your generosity and quiet courage were a light in the darkest hours.

To **Odessa O'Meara** and **Rob Charlton**—I am very thankful for your quick and decisive actions. You were there in my most critical moment, and I will be forever grateful.

With all my heart, I extend my deepest gratitude to every staff member who was on duty at CCMHA on the morning of July 22, 2022. Your care, presence, and dedication made all the difference. I will never forget it.

To my family—my brothers: **Clement**, **Fredrick**, and **Adeyemi**, and their incredible wives **Olayemi**, **Olanike**, and **Damilola**, and to my beloved mother, **Alice Kehinde Aderinto**—your prayers, faith, and love crossed oceans and borders to reach me. I felt your strength every single day.

To my sister-in-law, **Chidiogo Okeke**—without hesitation, you welcomed my children into your home for a week, giving them comfort, care, and stability. You asked for nothing and gave everything. Thank you.

To everyone who came to visit me in the hospital — thank you from the bottom of my heart.

Some of you showed up even before I was awake. Some of you were turned away at the door because of COVID rules, but I still felt your love.

I'm truly grateful for every single one of you.

Sandra Nasheim — you drove over two hours just to be by my side. That means more than words can say. I am grateful.

Jay Luistro, Rita McDonald's, and **Leni Patterson** — your presence brought a smile to my face. Seeing you reminded me of the beauty of friendship and the strength of connection.

Adriana Quezada Pérez — you came not just once, but on many days. Your kindness and presence brought light to me. Thank you.

To the medical team at **Foothills Medical Center, Calgary**—I benefited from your minds, hands and hearts. Thank you for your skills, your kindness, and care.

On the road to recovery, I met many angels. One of the brightest among them was **Dr. Ricky Wai Kee Kwok.**

Dr. Kwok is more than a doctor—he is a rare kind of human being. He treats each patient not as a case, but as a whole person, with integrity, compassion, and sincere empathy. When I left the hospital, I thought that might be the end of our connection. But Dr. Kwok didn't let go. He followed up, personally guiding me to a rehabilitation center where I could rebuild my strength and start reclaiming my life.

Even when I returned to work, he kept checking in—not just on my physical health, but on my quality of life. He asked about driving, family, rest, hobbies—details that most wouldn't think to ask. But he did. Because he truly cared. Every patient deserves a Dr. Kwok—someone who sees beyond the medical chart and into the heart of the person they are helping to heal.

To the members of **Parallel Church in Claresholm**—your prayers, encouragement, and kindness held my family and me up. You were our quiet strength.

To my children—**Victoria**, **Vincent**, and **Victor**—you are my heart. This journey was hard on you, I know. But your resilience and love gave me reason to fight. I am so proud to be your mother.

To my husband, **Nnamdi Okeke**. I will never forget your hand in mine when I could not speak, the way you stood by me, unwavering, day after day. Your love gave me breath. Thank you

And to my **Father in Heaven**—every breath I take is Your gift. Your grace carried me when I had no strength. You surrounded me with love and wrapped me in purpose. Thank You for this life, and for every soul You placed along my path.

This book is for all of you—and for anyone who finds themselves in the fight of their life. May it remind you that you are never alone. With love, with faith, and with the people who stand beside us, we can rise, overcome, and thrive.

With all my heart,

Thank you.